VOLCANOES AND EARTHQUAKES

(Original French title:
*Volcans Séismes et Dérive
des Continents*)

by
Pierre Kohler

Photos by Katia Krafft

**Translated from the French by
Albert V. Carozzi and Marguerite Carozzi**

First English language edition published in 1987 by
Barron's Educational Series, Inc.

© 1986 Hachette S.A., 79, boulevard Saint-Germain, 75006 Paris

The title of the French edition is *Volcans Séismes et Dérive
des Continents.*

International Standard Book No. 0-8120-3832-0

Library of Congress Card No. 87-24132

PRINTED IN ITALY
890 9912 98765432

BARRON'S

New York • London • Toronto • Sydney

Contents

The Ballet of the Continents

So it is impossible to travel into the earth, and although the Kola Peninsula record may one day be broken, there is no reason to suppose that we could ever get very far below the earth's crust. What we know of the interior of the planet, we have learned from indirect measurements, based on the propagation of seismic waves. When an earthquake takes place somewhere at the surface of the globe, the shock waves it produces propagate, or spread out, in all directions at the surface as well as into the interior. After traveling some distance, the waves emerge several thousand kilometers from the earthquake and are recorded by seismographs, instruments that are sensitive to the slightest movement of the ground. With

Like Vulcan, *Roman god of both fire and metallurgy, volcanoes transform molten matter.*

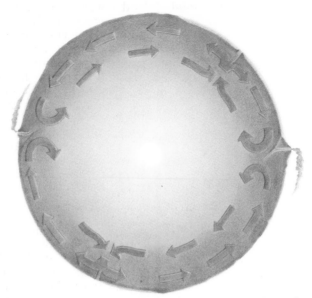

Heated by the earth's core, the magma of the mantle is subjected to convection currents that rise to the surface under the crust and thus cause the displacement of continental plates.

these instruments, the path of the waves can be reconstructed.

From the Surface to the Core

Scientists have been able to establish that well-defined layers exist in the earth's interior. We live on the solid, rocky skin which constitutes the earth's crust. Beneath the crust is the mantle; it is divided into an upper and a lower mantle. After that comes the core, encasing a kind of ball composed of iron and nickel, fourteen times denser than water. This ball is the "kernel," or internal core. It measures about 2500 kilometers (1550 miles) in diameter and reaches a temperature of 4300°C (7770°F). This is believed to be the prevailing temperature at the center of the earth, almost as high as the temperature on the surface of the sun (5700°C, or 10,300°F). Contrary to what might be expected, this kernel is not in a molten state but is very solid because of the very high pressures that prevail at the earth's center caused by the weight of the overlying layers.

The terrestrial core, including the kernel that it surrounds, represents only 14% of the volume and one third of the mass of the terrestrial globe. The other two-thirds correspond to the mantle, which is also the most voluminous part of our planet (83%). The skin or crust itself is insignificant; it is just a thin film enveloping the globe, its thickness varying from 6 kilometers (about 4 miles) under the oceans to 35 kilometers (about 22 miles) under the plains or the deserts, to 70 kilometers (45 miles) under the mountains. It consists basically of granite and volcanic rocks, like basalt. It weighs, in all, exactly 1% of the total weight of the earth.

An Everchanging Face

Although it is proportionately ten times thinner than an eggshell, the terrestrial crust is extremely important. It is the crust that gives the earth its multiple faces and so helps to make our planet the most varied and colorful in the whole solar system. In fact, nowadays the terrestrial crust and the upper mantle are no longer considered separate entities, for the two appear to be strongly linked. Indeed, it is in the upper mantle that many processes occur that give life to the crust and strongly influence the face of our planet. These include volcanoes, earthquakes, mountains, submarine trenches, and rift valleys.

All this becomes clear when we know that heat increases with depth. According to geophysicists, the geothermal gradient for the earth is on the average 1° every 30 meters (100 feet). This means that the temperature is already 100° at a depth of only 3000 meters (10,000 feet). At about 35 kilometers (22 miles) the temperature of 1000° is sufficient for rocks to reach their melting point. There the fluid zone of the mantle is reached.

This structure of the earth is rather like that of a fruit of which the skin would be the crust, the pulp the mantle, and the kernel the core. What is most interesting, however, as we have seen, is what happens

How old is the earth?

The earth assumed its size and almost spherical shape about 4650 million years ago. This has been deduced from analysis of the oldest materials found in the solar system — that is, meteorites. All the planets were formed out of a cloud of rock and metal dust surrounding the sun, and the meteorites are remains of that cloud. The lunar specimens brought back by the astronauts of the Apollo missions are also 465 billion years old.

On the moon, matter of that age can still be found because that celestial body has evolved very little. The earth, on the other hand, is a living planet. Its surface has been recarved several times since it began, because the oceanic ridges generate new crust while the old one is remelted when it sinks back into the mantle. However, in the heart of the continents, where the terrestrial crust is thicker, rocky masses exist that have essentially not sunk. These are the "cratons." They occur in Canada, South Africa, Greenland, Scandinavia, and Australia and display the oldest rocks in the world — 3.6 billion years old (in Labrador and Greenland). Geologists believe that the crust of our planet has been solid for only 3.8 billion years. Therefore, the first 900 million years of the history of the earth have been erased forever.

between pulp and skin—in other words, between mantle and crust. This zone is in fact neither too fluid nor too solid but just viscous enough to allow the large plates forming the terrestrial skin (see the next chapter) to slide over its surface. This zone, called the asthenosphere, extends to about 700 kilometers (440 miles). It transmits toward the surface slow convection currents, which are to some degree mixtures of matter caused by the intense heat of the interior of the globe. This hot matter has, indeed, a tendency to rise; but as it does so, it cools off and then plunges back into the depths of the planet, where it heats up again, and so on. These slowly swirling masses, which, it must be realized, move slowly, force the large plates (called "tectonic plates") on which the continents rest, to move relative to one another. Some plates, moving away from each other, form oceans; others colliding and folding give birth to great mountain chains; and others sink to become large submarine trenches.

So, on a time scale that is very long compared with a human life but very short compared with the history of the earth, the continents can be seen to move and the sea floor to renew itself unceasingly. Our earth is a changing planet that did not always have its present face. Over some hundreds of thousands of years from now, our present geographic atlases will no longer be valid.

It takes 3 days of walking to reach this plateau, above which rise Mounts Mawenzi and Kibo in Kenya. These peaks of volcanic origin reach 4400 meters (14,400 feet), which is the elevation of the highest Alpine peaks.

Drifting Continents

Take an atlas of the world and look at it closely. Any good observer cannot fail to notice that the Atlantic coast of South America fits almost exactly into the coast of Africa, which faces it. Almost like two pieces of a puzzle, the tip of northeastern Brazil fits perfectly into the Gulf of Guinea.

This fit was noticed in 1912 by Alfred Wegener, a young German astronomer and meteorologist. In January of that year, at a meeting in Hamburg, he presented his most revolutionary theory for the first time. He stated that today's continents did not always occupy the same position they do now and that they had drifted with respect to one another on the surface of the globe.

Wegener developed this hypothesis at greater length in a book called *The Origin of Continents and Oceans*, published in 1925. This book was such a success that it was revised and reprinted three times before Wegener died accidentally, during an expedition to a polar island off Greenland. In support of his theory, the German scientist pointed out not only the near-perfect fit of South America with Africa, but also the fact that rocks, as well as fossil plants and animals, were identical on both sides of the ocean. In particular, *Mesosaurus*, a sharp-toothed lizard, 30 to 40 centimeters (12 to 16 inches) long, lived both in Brazil and in what are now the countries of West Africa about 250 million years ago. Geologic and fossil similarities could also be found between Argentina and Botswana. Everything seemed to prove that these regions had formerly been joined.

Mountains at the Bottom of the Ocean

Wegener's theory was completely rejected at the time.

When India, a large island that had been separated from Africa, collided with the Asian continent, mountains were raised! *In fact, from this impact, which took place some 60 million years ago, were born the highest peaks in the world—those of the Himalayas—and also the plateaus of Tibet, a country of sages and holy men devoted to meditation and prayer rather than war. (above, The Paradise of Amithaba, a painting on cloth.)*

Not until 1960 when the American geologist, Harry Hess discovered seafloor spreading, did it begin to be accepted. Soon afterwards, evidence for this theory accumulated quickly. For example, fossils of trilobites of the same age were found in Norway, Scotland, and Ireland, on the one hand, and in Newfoundland on the other; here was proof that the North Atlantic had not always existed and that it was less than 400 million years old, the age of these fossils. Also, a map of the ocean floor, drawn with the help of instruments called "sonars" (a kind of submarine radar), clearly showed the existence of a long chain of mountains winding under the sea from Iceland to Antarctica, almost exactly halfway between the Americas on one side and Europe and Africa on the other.

When submarine cartography was extended to the other oceans it revealed that this mountain chain (called the midoceanic ridge) does not merely separate the Atlantic into two parts but also extends into the other oceans (Pacific and Indian Oceans). It branches into a Y-shape and then meets again, after having outlined

on the bottom of the seas a garland 64,000 kilometers (40,000 miles) long.

A more exhaustive exploration of this ridge in the North Atlantic revealed that there were in fact not one, but two, parallel mountain ranges, separated by a trench 20 to 50 kilometers (about 12 to 30 miles) wide—the midoceanic "rift". Geophysicists then realized that magma coming from the mantle was flowing out, very slowly through this sort of "lip." This explains why heat flow of the earth's crust is 10 times greater in the middle of the oceans and why it diminishes when approaching the continents. At the same time, geophysicists realized that islands and archipelagos spread along the track of these midoceanic ridges (Iceland, the Azores, and Saint Helena, for instance, in the Atlantic) represent only the peaks of this submarine range; they are slightly higher than the other peaks and emerge therefore from the ocean. The average height of these submarine summits is no more than 2000 meters (6500 feet), whereas the average depth of the Atlantic is 3600 meters (almost 12,000 feet).

Wegener Was Right

At last everything had become perfectly clear: through the "lips" of the midoceanic faults flows magma, which immediately solidifies but is constantly pushed away by a new flow. Therefore, the sea floor increases on both sides of the ridge and consequently, it pushes apart continents that used to be joined, like South America and Africa. When the age

On the east bank of Lake Abhe (Territory of Djibouti) rise these small volcanic vents, which still sometimes spit out sulfurous vapors.

11

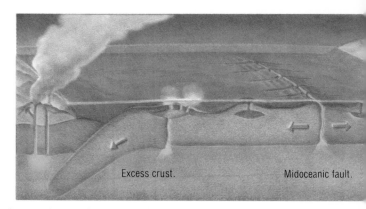

Excess crust.

Midoceanic fault.

Starting from midoceanic faults or continental "rifts," the earth's surface is increased by the flow of lava. Elsewhere excess crust disappears, sinking under a previously formed plate.

of rocks collected at the bottom of the ocean was measured, it was observed that the farther they are from the ridge the older they are.

Where do the continents go that are pushed back in this way? The surface of our planet being limited, there obviously cannot be a continuous generation of solid crust. The answer is simple: when oceanic floors meet a denser continental plate, they plunge under that plate, sinking into the asthenosphere, where they melt. This is what the experts call "subduction." What is generated on one side is thus remelted or undone on the other. The exception is when two continents collide. Since they have exactly the same density, neither will give way and a shock occurs. Forced against each other, the two rocky plates fold and form a mountain range. This is what happened, for instance, 40 million years ago, when North Africa collided with Europe. The thrust of Morocco against Spain gave birth to the Pyrenees; that of Tunisia and Libya pushing against Italy created the Alps. This movement is still going on, so that Mont Blanc and the Pelvoux, for instance, are uplifted 1 to 2 millimeters a year. This uplift is not a lot;

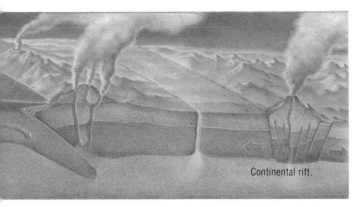

Continental rift.

these peaks will rise only 1 meter (3 feet) in seven centuries. It is enough, however, to generate severe earthquakes, as we shall see, in Italy, Yugoslavia, and Algeria, as well as in Provence, France. For the same reason, the Straits of Gibraltar will be closed a million years from now and the Mediterranean will no longer communicate with the Atlantic.

So Alfred Wegener was right. Continents move on the surface of the earth, and the global geography of the planet changes, over some millions or tens of millions of years. Since 1967, no scientist has doubted that these changes take place, but it has to be said that the relatively simple theory of the German scientist has

been considerably expanded. Today it is called "plate tectonics." This means that continents do not really float on the mantlelike rafts, as Wegener believed. Instead, scientists believe that a certain number of solid plates are in motion. These plates are fragments of the terrestrial crust or lithosphere, and support the continents and their adjacent half-oceans. There is one exception however— the Pacific Ocean, the bottom of which is a single plate in itself.

There are thirteen plates, seven large and six small. The seven main plates support Eurasia (Europe and Asia), North America, South America, Africa, Indo-Australia (India, Australia, and part of the

Unusual view: *the terrestrial globe defined, like a giant puzzle, by its continental plates.*

Indian Ocean), Antarctica, and the Pacific. These plates, which are 70 to 100 kilometers (45 to 65 miles) thick, slide over the magma of the asthenosphere, the latter representing the upper part of the mantle. Using a much simplified image we may say that the surface of the earth looks somewhat like a tortoise shell, with the difference that the scales are movable.

Huge Blocks in Movement

Today's scientists have succeeded in tracing quite precisely the history of these great plates and in finding their past positions. We can go back almost 600 million years. Then, a single continent, "Pangaea," existed at the surface of the earth, surrounded by a vast ocean called the "Tethys Sea." This single block contained all the present continents. It occupied a position such that the Sahara, 440 million years ago, was located where the South Pole is now.

About 220 million years ago, Pangaea began to break up into two sub-blocks: Gondwana (which corresponds approximately to the continents of the present southern hemisphere) and Laurasia (the northern hemisphere). At that time, the two poles were in open sea, and this gave rise to a long period of warm climates favorable to the development of the reptiles.

About 160 million years ago, the formation of the South Atlantic began, with Africa separating from South America and Antarctica beginning to drift toward the South Pole, to assume its present position. India, for its part, began its migration to the north, which, after a journey of 7000 kilometers (4500 miles) would collide with Asia, over which it would be thrust, causing the formation of the highest mountain range in the world, the Himalayas. As for Europe, it rotated and placed itself opposite North Africa. The North Atlantic, caused by the separation of Europe from North America, was not to form until later, since the beginning of that separation took place only 80 million years ago.

The "Children" of Pangaea

One may wonder what stage of development life on earth had reached at that time. When Pangaea began to break up, we were at the beginning of the Mesozoic Era, in a period that geologists call Triassic (220 million years ago). This is quite a long time compared with human history (which goes back only 3 million years) but short compared with the age of our planet—the equivalent of 1 hour and 10 minutes in a day of 24 hours.

At that time, flowering plants did not exist, only ferns and conifers. The only animals were fish, insects, and reptiles. There

Continental stock-car racing

Seven large plates share the surface of the planet:
— The North American plate (including Greenland), which stretches east to the middle of the Atlantic and stops on the other side at the edge of the Pacific.
— The South American plate, which also stretches from the Pacific coast (Andes cordilleras) to the middle of the Atlantic.
— The Pacific plate, the only one that is exclusively oceanic.
— The Eurasian plate, which meets the North American plate in the middle of the Atlantic. Its southern edge corresponds to a fault that crosses the Mediterranean and continues to the east through Turkey and the Himalayas.
— The African plate extends from the middle of the South Atlantic to the coast of the Indian Ocean.
— The Indo-Australian plate consists of Arabia, India, the eastern half of the Indian Ocean, and Australia.
— The Antarctic plate.

There are also six other, smaller, plates that are less well known. These are the Nazca, Cocos, Caribbean, and Philippine plates and the Aegean and Arabian plates. All these plates move at different speeds. The record for speed is held by the small Cocos plate, which is sinking under the North American continent at a rate of 10 centimeters (4 inches) a year; the sinking of the Nazca plate under South America takes place at a slightly slower speed. In contrast, the movement between the large South American plate and the small Caribbean plate is not even 1 centimeter (½ inch) a year.

Today.

Equator   38 million years ago.

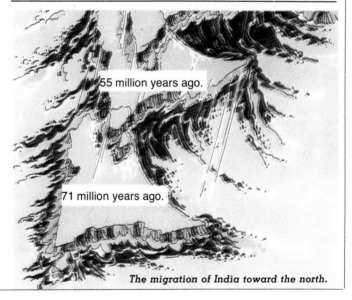

55 million years ago.

71 million years ago.

The migration of India toward the north.

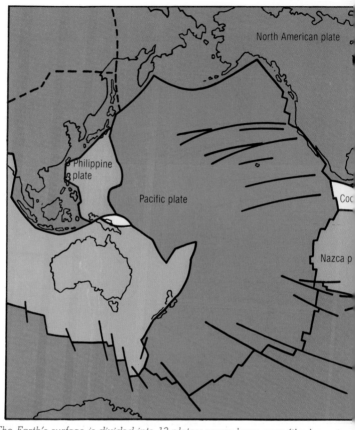

The Earth's surface is divided into 13 plates: seven large ones (the largest corresponding to the Pacific) and six small ones.

were no birds yet, nor mammals, but it was the beginning of the reign of the dinosaurs. Mammals appeared in the middle of the Mesozoic Era, about 160 million years ago, when the South Atlantic opened up, but they did not really flourish until the formation of the North Atlantic, when America separated from Europe, 80 million years ago. Then, when Africa began to collide with Europe some 65

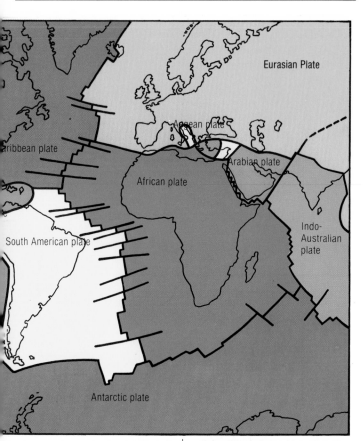

million years ago, the reign of the dinosaurs came to an end rather quickly.

Shortly thereafter, India collided with Asia, causing a plateau to arise that is today Tibet. All this happened very slowly, and much later (30 million years ago) strange mammals like Indricotherium, a kind of giant rhinoceros, could be found grazing on the plains of northern India. The formation of the Himalayas, previously mentioned, took place a little later. The Himalayan peaks, including Everest, the highest of all, continue to rise.

19

The Earth's Tremors

According to a thousand-year-old legend, the whole Japanese archipelago rests on the back of a "namazu" — a large catfish (see below). A god called Daimyogin, armed with a mallet, is watching it to see that it doesn't move. Alas, from time to time the god's attention wanders and the fish wiggles its spine, making all Japan tremble. Obviously, nobody believes this story of the catfish any more. Several times a year, earthquakes cause damage or claim victims in various places on the planet, and geophysicists now know exactly the cause of these tremors of the terrestrial crust.

In Sicily, in the neighborhood of Etna, the destruction wrought by volcanic eruptions is sometimes increased by that of frequent earthquakes in this unstable region of the Mediterranean basin.

There are three kinds of earthquakes. The most frequent are a natural consequence of continental drift. We have seen that the continents are, in fact, carried by vast rocky plates that move slowly with respect to one another. These movements, consisting of displacements of a few centimeters a year, cannot take place smoothly, given the hardness of rocks. Forces accumulate underground until a rupture occurs. This return to equilibrium causes a tremor, the vibrations of which spread to the surface, shaking everything on it. The point of rupture is the *hypocenter*, or focus, and the one just above, at ground level, is the *epicenter*.

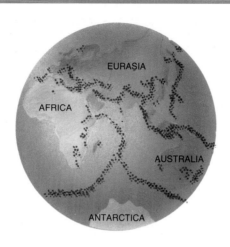

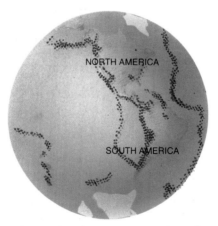

Location of the main earthquake epicenters on the surface of the planet.

Major Types of Earthquakes

When two continental plates collide, as in the case of the subcontinent of India, which was thrust against Asia, particularly violent earthquakes occur. This collision is the origin of the many deadly earthquakes affecting China.

The earthquakes recorded around the Pyrenees, which are fortunately less violent, or south of the Alps (in northern Italy and Yugoslavia) are caused in the same way—by the slow pressure of Africa against Europe. These two folded mountain belts are zones of weakness.

Strong earthquakes also happen above *subduction zones*—that is, where a light plate sinks under a denser plate. Such is the case of Japan, which is situated right above the line where the Pacific plate sinks under Asia. The sinking of this same Pacific plate under South America is likewise responsible for earthquakes affecting the Cordilleras of the Andes, Chile in particular. These earthquakes caused by the displacement of continents are called *tectonic* earthquakes.

There are also volcanic earthquakes. As their name indicates, they accompany or precede volcanic eruptions. They are caused by the sporadic rise of magma in volcanic vents. These tremors are seldom strong.

Finally, the third category consists of earthquakes caused by land-slides, either terrestrial or submarine, or by the collapse of caves. Earthquakes of this type are often caused by human beings. Frequently, for instance, the filling of dams by significantly overloading weak rocks, or by the infiltration of water into fissures, sets off small earthquakes.

Unending Earthquakes

Contrary to appearances, no quiet periods exist that are not interrupted by earthquakes. In reality, as can be demonstrated by modern ultrasensitive seismographic recording of the earth's tremors in more than 700 places around the world, our planet shakes almost continuously. Each year, all over the world, more than 200 earthquakes are detected by humans, whereas several tens of thousands are not.

Earthquakes with the deepest foci (from 650 to 700 kilometers, or 400 to 440 miles) occur at the edge of oceanic trenches, where one continental plate sinks under another. None have been detected below 700 kilometers (440 miles), which indicates that, at that depth, the rocks have become fluid, have melted into the mantle, and therefore can no longer cause friction. Earthquakes that occur between 300 and 700 kilometers (190 and 440 miles) are considered deep; those between 70 and 300 kilometers (45 and 190 miles) are called intermediate, and those of less than 70 kilometers (45 miles) superficial.

Most earthquakes that cause severe damage occur, in fact, less than 5 kilometers (3 miles) below the surface. Three quarters of the total energy liberated by earthquakes over the entire world results from shocks that occurred at depths less than these first five kilometers. The focus of the terrible Agadir earthquake in Morocco, which caused 25,000 deaths on February 29, 1960, was situated right under the city at a very shallow depth. This is why the city was entirely destroyed.

There is also the question of "aftershocks." This is the name given to tremors that are very numerous but usually less intense, occurring during the days, weeks, and sometimes even months after a great earthquake. During the 24-hour period after a serious earthquake that took place on February 14, 1965, on Rat Island in the middle of the Aleutian Archipelago, 750 of these were counted. After the deadly earthquake at El Asnam in Algeria, on October 10, 1980, a total of 6000 aftershocks were counted over 6 months. The Friuli earthquake in Italy on May 6, 1975, was followed by another severe shock 5 months later, with thousands of small tremors occurring in the meantime.

Catastrophes Within Recorded History

All these earthquakes together release energy each year, all over the earth, equivalent to about 10 million small atomic bombs. The zones affected by these shocks vary in size according to the intensity of the earthquake and the depth of the focus.

The record seems to be held by the Lisbon earthquake of November 1, 1755. It was described in detail by Voltaire. This earthquake, estimated at a magnitude of 9 on the Richter scale, shook a surface of 40 million square kilometers, more than 70 times the surface of France.

The Mino-Owari earthquake of October 28, 1891, in the center of Japan, was also very severe. Not only did it destroy 142,000 houses and cause 7000 deaths but it also left deep scars on the land, with a vertical slip of 3 meters (10 feet) on the fault and a horizontal slip of 8 meters (25 feet).

After the severe earthquake that destroyed San Francisco almost entirely on April 18, 1906 (it was felt within a radius of 1200 kilometers), slips of 6 meters

California is one of the most dangerous regions of the United States. This is because of the San Andreas Fault, a tear in the earth's crust. In some tens of millions of years, California will be an island off the coast of North America. (Map and satellite picture.)

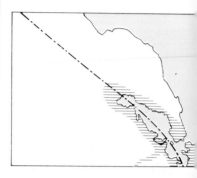

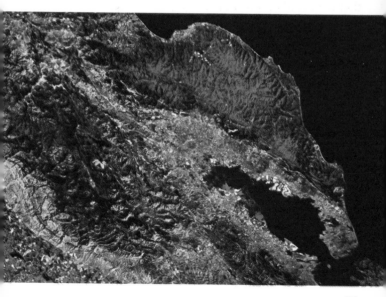

(20 feet) were noticed along the San Andreas Fault, responsible for the earthquakes affecting this region of California. The San Andreas Fault is indeed quite clearly visible from the air, like a long gash in the plain of Carizo, between Los Angeles and San Francisco.

An earthquake in itself does not last long, rarely more than 15 seconds, but these few seconds must seem an eternity to those who experience the cataclysm. Tremors sometimes last for a minute, but this is a maximum and very rare.

The great majority of seismic waves propagate horizontally. When they are not too violent, they make dishes rattle in cupboards or cause chandeliers to swing. If the earthquake is very severe, then the walls of buildings crumble.

However, sometimes seismic waves propagate vertically. In such cases, poles are uprooted from the ground. The Assam earthquake in India, on June 12, 1897, even threw people

This dislocated road is the result of a volcanic earthquake. It is the effect of Mauna Loa in Hawaii. In November 1983, the whole island was shaken by a very strong earthquake (magnitude 6.6) that had its focus under the southeast side of this active volcano.

An impressive fault formed by an earthquake at Hokkaido (Japan) in August 1977.

into the air who were injured when they fell back. During the earthquake at Imaichi in Japan, on December 26, 1949, stones 50 centimeters (20 inches) in diameter were ejected into the air several times in a row, bouncing like balls. Potatoes were even dug up in this way, again in Japan, during the Kwanto earthquake of September 1, 1923.

The Earth as a Killer

Most often damage and death are caused not by the earthquake itself but by the catastrophes it unleashes: landslides and mudflows, avalanches, falling objects, floods from the breeching of dikes and dams, tsunamis (erroneously called tidal waves), and fires. For instance, most of the 60,000 victims of the Lisbon earthquake were drowned by the powerful tsunami that followed it. In the same way, the urban areas of Tokyo-Yokohama in 1923 and of San Francisco in 1906 were almost entirely destroyed because of fires started by the earthquakes, not by the earthquakes.

Dangerous tsunamis

An earthquake located near a coastline or under the sea can unleash an event even more deadly than the earthquake itself. It is a huge wave, called by its Japanese name tsunami and indeed such waves are frequent in Japan. About 150 of them are counted per year. The Pacific coast is the most exposed.
At the point of origin, the oscillation of the water has a wavelength so large (sometimes 100 kilometers, or 60 miles, from crest to crest) that it remains unnoticed. A boat can navigate between the two crests without being aware of them. When the wave reaches a shore and the depth diminishes, however, it narrows, rises, and finally breaks onto land with all its might. The waterside inhabitants then face a wall of water moving toward them, which may be 25 to 35 meters (80 to 110 feet) high. Some of the largest tsunamis have reached 40 meters (125 feet). Their power is such that they can carry small boats for several miles inland. Needless to say, they destroy everything in their path. Sometimes, before the arrival of a tsunami, there is a seiche effect: the sea suddenly withdraws, uncovering a large sandy beach. Some minutes later it returns violently as a monstrous wave.

not by the earthquake itself.

Whether they act directly or indirectly, earthquakes are very deadly and are responsible for an average of 2500 deaths a year, but there are great differences from year to year. In the year 1976 alone, for instance, more than 650,000 persons died in the Chang Chan earthquake in China, and 50,000 were killed elsewhere, for a total of 700,000 deaths — as many as in all the 75 preceding years. Many countries were hit in 1976, including China, Chile, Guatemala, the Philippines, Turkey, and Italy. Not for more than four centuries had earthquakes claimed so many victims in the same year, not since the absolute record held by the earthquake that hit China in 1556 and caused 830,000 deaths.

The Wave of Kanagawa, as seen by the Japanese artist Hokusai.

A Difficult Forecast

Because these shivers of the earth have such consequences, scientists make great efforts to try to forecast them. A certain number of early warnings are known, but it is difficult to study them systematically. Considering the immensity of the zones to be covered, it would mean setting up numerous measuring instruments. In particular, it would be necessary to measure the speed of wave propagation in the ground (it decreases by 15% before a tremor), or the emission of radon (an inert gas) from wells and faults.

A more empirical method, but one that sometimes proves useful, consists of observing the behavior of animals. Just before an earthquake, hens fly into trees; ducks come out of the water; dogs bark savagely; and pigs, surprisingly, become strangely calm. Snakes and rodents leave their lairs.

It was in this way that the Chinese were able to forecast 24 hours in advance an earthquake that took place on February 4, 1975, in the northeast of the country. The villages of Yuigkon and Anshan and some others in the area were evacuated. No one was there when a violent earthquake struck the whole area, demolishing nine houses in ten.

Unfortunately, no one was able to forecast the earthquake that, on July 27 of the following year, left 630,000 dead at Tangshan, east of Peking.

Recently, as here in Tokyo, the Japanese have learned to build flexible towers capable of resisting a very strong earthquake.

The Richter scale

Almost in the same way that meteorologists use a temperature scale to follow the evolution of climate, geophysicists have at their disposition a scale for evaluating the energy unleashed by an earthquake. This scale is called Richter after its inventor. It has neither a minimum threshold (everything depends on the sensitivity of the seismograph) nor a maximum one. Thus the weakest earthquakes detected have a negative magnitude, like −2 °C temperatures. The strongest ever recorded was the Lisbon earthquake in 1755: it must have had a magnitude of 9 on the Richter scale. Unlike the temperature scale, the Richter scale is not proportional, because energy multiplies by 30 each time it increases one magnitude. Therefore an earthquake of magnitude 4 releases 30 times more energy than an earthquake of magnitude 3. For a magnitude of 5 the ratio is $30 \times 30 = 900$ times greater!

Scientists also use a scale of intensity (called the MKS scale), which is not so well known to the public and which indicates the extent of the damage done at the epicenter. Certainly this intensity depends on the energy, but also on the depth of the focus, and on the nature of the rocks, which can more or less absorb the waves. The MKS scale consists of twelve degrees.

The Fire in the Earth

The earth shakes and splits up. Gases and flames shoot out. Perhaps, soon lava will come. (on the right): a volcano is beginning to erupt. For how long? What intensity will this event reach? It is very difficult to answer such questions. For a volcano is somewhat like a human being. It can calm down, go dormant, then wake up all of a sudden, sometimes after a very long sleep of several thousand years or more.

On the morning of February 20, 1943, a Mexican farmer was much surprised to see his field being torn in two, like a piece of paper. What escaped from the tear first was fine ash, then water vapor, and last molten rocks, ejected violently into the air.

By noon, a mound of rocks 30 meters (100 feet) high had formed in the field, and by evening a first flow of lava — that is, of molten rocks — was coming out of the mound. A volcano had just been born in the middle of the countryside 320 kilometers (200 miles) west of Mexico City. A year later, to the very day, the volcano was 340 meters (1100 feet) high and its lava had buried the villages of Paricutin and San Juan, only the church of which rose higher than the lava field. After 9 years of activity, Paricutin subsided but there is a strong likelihood that it will someday wake up again.

After a Long Sleep

In November 1963, in the sea off Iceland, a new volcano erupted that is now called Surtsey. From the ship that first saw it it looked at first like another ship burning. A week later this new volcanic island was 70 meters (225 feet) high. The volcano reached 150 meters (500 feet) and then calmed down, after 4 years of activity. It too will doubtless awaken some day.

Another volcanic island,

Heimaey, on the south coast of Iceland, awoke in just the same way on January 23, 1973, after a dormant period of 5000 years. In fact, it formed a second cone, Helgafell, 800 meters (2650 feet) from the first one. In France, the last eruption of Pavin, one of the numerous volcanoes in the Auvergne, occurred 3500 years ago. Perhaps these volcanoes are completely extinct; perhaps they will soon awaken. No one knows. Vesuvius had been dormant for 1000 years when the celebrated and deadly eruption took place in 79 A.D. that was to bury Herculaneum and Pompeii near Naples, and the eruption of Mount Saint Helens, in the United States, one of the most powerful of recent years, interrupted a quiet sleep that had lasted 123 years.

The most active volcano is the Piton de la Fournaise (2631 meters) on the island of Réunion. It has had eighty eruptions since the beginning of the century. During the same period, Kilauea and Mauna Loa, on the Hawaiian islands, have experienced fifty and forty eruptions, respectively, which is also a lot. Aso in

Japan and Etna in Sicily also awaken quite often, about every 5 years on the average. All these volcanoes can be considered active. When they no longer spit anything up, it is just because they are dormant.

There are some volcanoes that never rest—like Stromboli to the north of the Sicilian coast, which erupts regularly, every 20 minutes.

When Humanity Awakens Volcanoes

It has sometimes happened that humans have awakened volcanoes, either deliberately or accidentally. The first time, in 1919, a sulfur mine at the foot of Popocatepetl, the volcano that dominates Mexico City, was dynamited to make mining operations easier. The charge

The Pavlof (Alaska) is one of the most active volcanoes in North America: it has awakened twenty-six times since 1700. Its last eruption was in 1976.

was very weak but it was enough to bring on the collapse of the internal wall, which in turn cracked the floor. A dome of lava then rose and buried the mine.

During World War II, an American pilot, returning from a bombing mission, released two unused bombs in the very middle of the crater of dormant Vesuvius. A small volcanic cone then formed at the bottom. Luckily, the charges were not sufficient to awaken the volcano completely and unleash a catastrophe.

Finally, in 1977, geologists bored holes in Krafla to open a geothermal well using the heat of the volcano. The magma, however, used one of the holes to flow toward the exterior and nearly 3 tons of lava spread before solidifying.

To sum up, it can be seen that the task of making a volcano erupt under control is difficult. The power we command is often laughable against the sheer volume of these monsters of nature.

The Movie of an Eruption

When a volcano is about to erupt, small earthquakes

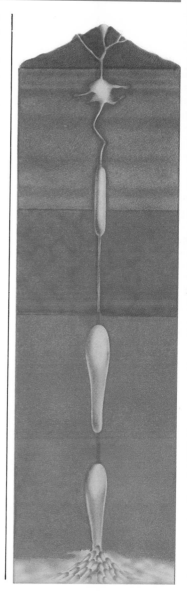

are felt in the area, in the few preceding days. They are generated by the rising of the magma in the vent, for this rise takes place by successive jolts. Then the shaking stops and everything becomes still again, but it is a deceptive stillness for the eruption is then imminent. Deformations of the volcanic cone, swollen by the thrust of the magma, can also be observed. During the great eruption of Mount Saint Helens in 1980, the northern flank of the volcanic cone rose several meters during the preceding weeks. Then the whole area was blown away by the explosion.

A volcanic eruption is a very noisy event. The one at Coseguina in Nicaragua, in 1835, was heard as far as Colombia. The 1883 explosions of Krakatoa awakened Australians 3000 kilometers (1875 miles)

Real bubbles of very hot magma rise slowly through the mantle (on the left). In the lower part of the terrestrial crust, these solid bubbles, which assume an elongated shape, supply magmatic chambers from which the lava pushes its way to the surface by forming more or less ramified volcanic vents (below).

Color and temperature

It is possible to tell the temperature of lava by its color. This temperature varies between 1550-2300°F—dark red up to 1650°F, light red from 1650 to 1900°F, orange from 1900 to 2100°F, and yellow above that. The lava's fluidity depends on its

chemical composition and also on its temperature. From 1800 to 1950°F, lava is only partly molten and remains stiff. Below 1800°F it is hard, and above 1950°F completely fluid. In any case, these rocks retain heat so well that a flow 1 meter (3 feet) thick takes a month to cool; a flow of 20 meters (70 feet) takes a year!

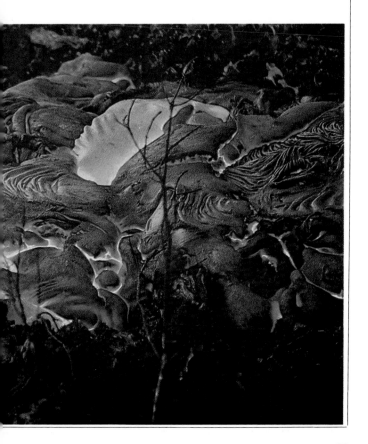

These ropy lavas (called pahoe hoe), *covered by a thin vitreous layer, formed on the sides of the* Piton de la Fournaise *on Réunion.*

away. These same explosions broke windows within a radius of 500 kilometers (300 miles) and were thought by English sailors, who were cruising near the island of Rodriguez in the Indian Ocean, to be cannons firing. The distance was 4800 kilometers (3000 miles)! The sound reached the sailors' ears 4 hours after the eruption occurred.

Magma rises in the vent (less than 1 kilometer an hour), and when it gushes into the air it is called lava. Depending on the type of volcano, lava can have either a smooth surface or a rugged or a blocky one.

Smooth lava flows like hot chocolate and forms sausagelike *bodies* when it cools. This is what happened at the Piton de la Fournaise (Réunion Island). Rugged lava is thicker, and forms *scoria,* which advances like heaps of stones pushed by a mechanical shovel. This can be seen at Etna in Sicily. When the lava comes out in blocks, it is very thick and advances by successive rock falls, forming a jumble of huge, angular blocks, like those seen at the foot of Sakurajima, in Japan. When this lava erupts under water, as it does in submarine volcanoes, it solidifies into pillow-shaped bodies.

Traveling Ash

A volcano is not just a flow of lava; it also ejects fine and coarse ash *lapilli* (stones the size of a tennis ball), and sometimes even giant blocks of stone weighing several tons. Coarse volcanic ash is the same size as grains of sand and falls fairly quickly; however, fine ash can climb very high and be carried off by stratospheric currents. The fine ash from Mount Saint Helens reached an altitude of 18 kilometers (11 miles), and that from El Chichon (which awoke in Mexico in 1982) 35 kilometers (22 miles). The record seems to be held by the fine ash of Krakatoa, which in 1883 reached 40 kilometers (25 miles). Certain scientists evaluate the altitude reached by the fine ash of Taupo, a New

Augustine, an Alaskan volcano that started erupting in 1976, simultaneously ejected pyroclastic flows (nuées ardentes) and mudflows.

Only the tower of the cathedral of Paricutin in Mexico *emerges from blocky lava, which buried an entire village in 1943.*

Zealand volcano that awoke in the year 186 A.D. as 50 kilometers (30 miles).

At such altitudes, these ash clouds take several years to fall back to earth and therefore go around the earth several times. Ash from Krakatoa has been found in Antarctic ice. Ash from El Chichon was followed by the cameras of weather satellites. This particular cloud took 20 days to go around the earth, at an altitude of 25 kilometers (16 miles); it was moving at about 70 kilometers (45 miles) an hour.

Researchers sometimes find volcanic ash belonging to very ancient eruptions. For instance, materials ejected by the volcanoes of the Auvergne some thousands of years ago were found in the Vosges and in Belgium. The most astonishingly that of the volcano Toba, whose products, ejected 75,000 years ago, were found in the sediments of the island of Ceylon (now Sri Lanka).

Gases, Rocks, and Clouds

Besides fine and coarse ash, volcanoes give off incredible quantities of gases—water vapor, carbon dioxide, hydrogen, and sulfurous gas. It was volcanoes that, in the beginning, produced the primitive atmosphere of the earth. Mount Saint Helens in 5 months gave off 800,000 tons of carbon dioxide and 150,000 tons of

This drawing shows an eruption of Vesuvius in the nineteenth century. The last major eruption of this Italian volcano was in 1929.

sulfurous gas. Vesuvius in 1929 released into the atmosphere a million tons of water vapor in 1 day!

Perhaps Laki in Iceland holds the record. In 1783, it ejected 100 million tons of sufurous gas and 20 million tons of carbon dixoide. Laki also holds the record for the greatest lava flow—60 kilometers (nearly 40 miles). It is estimated that all the active volcanoes together release each year some tens of billion tons of gases.

More dangerous are the pyroclastic flows (*nuées ardentes*), truly avalanches of incandescent blocks mixed with ash and hot gases. They come to rest a few kilometers from the volcano and bury everything under them. Some, as

This street in Pompeii *is full of noise and life. One fine morning in the summer of 79 A.D., however, in just a few hours, the whole town was buried under several meters of hot ash ejected from nearby Vesuvius.*

at the Montagne Pelée (Martinique) in 1902 and Mount Saint Helens in 1980, are even expelled laterally and rush downward at the speed of a racing car. No one can escape this burning cloud.

The Last Days of Pompeii

During the first decades of the Christian era, Pompeii was a flourishing Roman city, existing peacefully at the foot of a mountain covered with pines, cypress, vineyards, and oleander. In the year 62, this tranquillity was disturbed by a small earthquake, but it was soon forgotten.

In the middle of August of the year 79, another earthquake affected the region, but this time it was more severe. For, some days later, on the morning of August 24, inhabitants who were outside their homes saw the mountain

explode and were immediately bombarded by hot *lapilli* and pumice stone. Those inside were soon to perish, buried under several meters of ash. This time Vesuvius was deeply angry. The explosion blew off the top of the whole summit, and an immense black cloud shot toward the sky, which darkened immediately and was streaked with lightning. Noon was transformed into night, and for 48 hours hot materials ejected from the volcano rained down continuously. Pompeii was buried under 6 meters (20 feet) of ash and pumice.

Some distance away, the villages of Herculaneum and Stabia were covered by a flow of molten matter that spread over the dwellings like a wave, reaching in some places a thickness of 20 meters (65 feet).

History took its course,

When volcanoes make aircraft cough

The most powerful volcanic eruptions create columns of gas and ash that can climb more than 20 kilometers (12 miles). Sometimes, flying through these clouds, jet engines choke. That means a plunge toward the earth is certain.

Of course, flying over volcanoes is forbidden, but it can happen that these clouds, carried far from the eruption by air currents, are penetrated by planes that do not see them for they become gradually diluted in the air. On June 24, 1982, a Boeing 747 belonging to a British company was flying between Malaysia and Australia at a height of 12,000 meters (40,000 feet) when the four engines cut out and an odor of sulfur pervaded the cockpit. At 4500 meters (15,000 feet), the pilot succeeded in restarting three of the jet engines and tried an emergency landing at Jakarta. The culprit was Mount Galunggung, in eruption on the island of Java, not far from there. On July 13 of the same year, a plane belonging to Singapore Airlines encountered the same difficulties, in the same area. On February 20, 1985, after a fall of 11,000 meters (37,000 feet), a China Airlines Boeing 747, crossing the Pacific toward Los Angeles, was barely able to resume its horizontal flight by the time it had almost reached ocean level. The volcano responsible for this accident has not yet been identified, but it should be recalled that the materials ejected by some volcanoes can travel around the world several times.

This young sulfur carrier *on the slopes of Popocatepetl, the largest Mexican volcano, reminds us that volcanoes can also be exploited for mineral resources.*

and the Roman cities and their thousands of inhabitants buried under the debris of Vesuvius were soon forgotten. It was not until fifteen centuries later, during terracing work being done for the routing of an aqueduct, that the ruins of Herculaneum and Pompeii were brought to light. After 1638, the two towns were gradually uncovered.

Following its great anger of the year 79, Vesuvius produced seven more severe eruptions, then remained silent for seven centuries, until 1766. Then, in less than 30 years it awoke nine times. Since then it has been dozing rather than dormant, its last big eruption occurring in 1906. It could very well fall into another great rage some years from now, a possibility that is all the more worrisome because more than 2 million people live on its perimeter. This is the largest known human concentration around an active volcano.

Not very far from there, in Sicily, there is Etna, which has also caused catastrophes—in 1669, it almost entirely buried the town of Messina. It regularly experiences worrying convulsions; the last two warnings occurred in August 1971 and October

Do volcanoes influence weather?

This question has been debated for a long time, but scientists agree now that volcanic eruptions definitely have an effect on the weather. However, the influence is clear only in the case of volcanoes that give off a lot of sulfur, as did the Mexican El Chichon in 1982. Calculations show that it ejected more than 3 million tons of sulfur. El Chichon was perhaps responsible for the rigors of the 1984–1985 winter. Although it ejected 100 times more dust than El Chichon, Mt. St. Helens, which erupted in 1980, did not have any noticeable effect on the weather.

Close examination of the meteorological records of the last century has confirmed that the weather was severely disturbed in the year 1816, the year following the eruption of Tambora (in Indonesia). Indeed, 1816 was called the year of no summer. Snow fell in June and frost occurred in August in the United Sates. Tambora was the largest volcanic eruption in the last 3000 years. Again, the 1883 eruption of Krakatoa in the same area gave rise to astonishing atmospheric effects over a large part of the earth for more than a year. In Europe, a strange light illuminated the night sky, so that one could read a newspaper at midnight. This was caused by the diffusion of solar light by fine particles of ash in suspension at high altitude.

At Lanzarotte (the Canaries archipelago) *these amazing funnel-shaped depressions have been dug to shelter vines and fig trees from the wind (which is very strong all year round). Without them, nothing would grow on these lava fields.*

1975. In vain do its lava flows bury houses and hotels built at its feet; humanity always returns and insists on living there. It must be said that volcanoes are, in certain countries, tourist attractions that bring in money. Apart from everything else, however, volcanic products are rich in minerals that yield particularly fertile land.

The Survivors of Saint Pierre

A catastrophe similar to the one at Pompeii hit the town of Saint Pierre (30,000 inhabitants) in Martinique on May 8, 1902. There, also, natural warnings were not lacking—for more than a month before clouds of gases had been coming out of the volcano, followed by some small earthquakes. The authorities reassured the population and maintained that the Montagne Pelée—the name of the volcano—would settle down. Indeed, the situation continued to get worse, and the noise of the volcano, which was spurting forth bigger and bigger blocks, was heard on the island of Guadeloupe. Suddenly all hell broke loose. In less

than 2 minutes, very early on that morning of May 8, a carpet of fire covered the town, coming at 160 kilometers (100 miles) an hour from a V-shaped gash that had just opened in the volcano's side. The pyroclastic flow (nuée ardente) overturned even the thickest walls and gutted casks of rum, which were set afire. Those who were not killed by the flames or falling debris from the houses perished by asphyxiation or were burned by air raised to a

temperature of more than 700°C (1300°F). In the harbor, sixteen of eighteen ships overturned under the weight of the blocks of rock thrown out by the volcano or caught fire.

Of the 30,000 inhabitants of Saint Pierre, only two survived this cataclysm — a sturdy shoemaker who was able to flee across the fields without getting too badly burned, and the town's one prisoner who owed his safety to the thickness of the walls of the jail. The tiny barred opening that communicated with the outer world prevented enough incandescent matter from penetrating the cell, but the prisoner was badly burned by the hot air. This miraculously escaped prisoner, Auguste Ciparis, was later pardoned and told his tale during tours of the Barnum Circus.

The splendor of Cretan civilization is displayed on this fresco. A gigantic tsunami, generated by the eruption of the volcano Thera, destroyed this civilization about 1500 B.C.

Exploding Volcanoes

Eruptions like those of Vesuvius or Mount Pelée are small, however, compared with the one experienced on Thera 3500 years ago.

This was, without a doubt, the most powerful eruption in historical times. Thera was situated in the Mediterranean 120 kilometers (75 miles) north of Crete and 200 kilometers (125 miles) south of Greece; its remains form the archipelago of Santorini. In the space of a few hours some tens of cubic kilometers of material were ejected. Thera literally exploded, giving rise to monstrous waves that devastated Crete and the coast of the Peloponnesus. The walls of water of this gigantic tsunami must, in places, have reached 40 meters (130 feet). This catastrophe occurred about 1450 B.C., according to dating of the deposits. No

Radial erosion *has carved the slopes of this extinct volcano in a strange way. It is called Batok, on the island of Java (Indonesia).*

written account has been found that would allow a dating more precise than within 50 years.

Many historians and oceanographers believe that the direct and indirect destruction caused by Thera was responsible for the disappearance of the Minoan civilization that inhabited Crete. This disappearance may be the origin of the legend of Atlantis. Of Thera, which must have been a mountain some 1500 meters (5000 feet) high, there remains only a crescent of four little islands emerging from the sea; they are all that is left of the walls of the former crater.

Two other very strong eruptions happened more recently—that of Tambora in 1815 and of Krakatoa in 1883, both in the Indonesian archipelago. Tambora, near the island of Bali, was 4000 meters (13,000 feet) high and was decapitated by a third of its height. The volume of rocks thrown into the air is estimated at 180 cubic kilometers, representing about 170 billion tons of materials—rocks, ash, and pumice stone. The toll was 92,000 dead, most having perished in the gigantic tsunami that fol-lowed, as in the case of Thera. The explosion of Krakatoa, although it was a little less powerful, is more famous. It was also less deadly, although it too was catastrophic: 36,000 dead in Java and Sumatra, again because of the tsunami generated by the eruption. In Ceylon, waves were still strong enough to beach fishing vessels, and a small additional tide was recorded in the gulf of Gascogne, 17,000 kilometers (11,000 miles) from the eruption. Of the volcanic island that had blocked the Sunda Strait, nothing remained but three rocky peaks jutting above the level of the ocean. In 1941, a new volcano formed in the interior of the old crater. It is called Anak-Krakatoa, son of Krakatoa.

The Awakening of Mount Saint Helens

The most powerful volcanic eruption of recent years was that of Mount Saint Helens, in the United States. Saint Helens, which roused itself on May 18, 1980, is one of the fifteen major volcanoes of the Cascades chain, which has experienced one large erup-

When volcanoes are unleashed, *they sow death and leave only desolation in their path. Life reclaims its rights very quickly, though, as can be seen from these peaceful landscapes (on the right), where fruit trees flourish at the foot of the dormant monster.*

tion per century over the last 10,000 years. This volcano is the most dangerous of the chain, and in fact its awakening had been expected sometime between now and the year 2000, its last violent explosion going back to 1857.

In a few hours, this part of the state of Washington, was changed into a lunar landscape. The summit of the mountain exploded under the violent thrust of the magma coming from the depths of the earth and was decapitated by 450

meters (1450 feet), giving birth to a crater 2 kilometers (over a mile) in diameter. The blast flattened all trees within 24 kilometers (15 miles) and a pyroclastic flow rushed down the north side at a rate of 370 kilometers (230 miles) an hour, killing 5000 deer, 1500 elk, 200 bears, and some imprudent tourists. In all, 500 square kilometers (125,000 acres) of woods, lakes, and grassland were devastated by the blast, the fires, and the 275 million tons of materials ejected from the volcano—more than a ton for every American.

The energy released at the height of the eruption, which lasted 9 hours, was the equivalent of the energy that would be released by

400 high-yield nuclear bombs. At Spokane, 430 kilometers (270 miles) downwind from the volcano, streets were covered with ash nearly a centimeter deep, and night arrived in the afternoon, visibility being no more than 30 meters (100 feet). Four more eruptions took place in the 5 months that followed, and then the volcano quieted down. It was astonishing that, just a few weeks after the last eruption, grasses and flowers reappeared. Life was reasserting itself.

After all these accounts, one might think that volcanic eruptions are the most deadly processes in the world. In fact, this is not so. Tsunamis, earthquakes, typhoons, and floods extract a heavier price.

Of course, it should be remembered that volcanoes are not just destructive. They create new landscapes and modify the face of the earth.

Can we fight volcanoes?

No one has ever yet tried to block the vent of a volcano. The energy that would be required and the amount of materials that would have to be supplied are just out of proportion to what human beings are capable of achieving. The power of a volcanic eruption is much greater than that of a nuclear bomb: the only difference is that volcanic energy is more spread out in time and does not produce the same effects.

Several times, however, people have been able to act quite effectively against lava flows exiting the mouth of a volcano — either by deflecting them or by cooling them. In May 1983, a flow from Etna that was threatening a Sicilian village was rerouted using dynamite. Earlier, in 1935 and in 1942, in the Hawaiian islands, the same effect was achieved by bombarding from an aircraft a flow of Mauna Loa. Good results have also been obtained by using walls of earth and rock constructed with the help of a bulldozer to deflect lava flows. This was done at Kilauea (also in the Hawaiian islands) in 1955. Also effective was the cooling of the flow of Helgafell, in Iceland, which was advancing along a front of 300 meters (1000 feet). From January 23, 1973, for several weeks forty-three pumps hooked to 30 kilometers (19 miles) of pipes, working day and night, were used to cool the lava with seawater; the cooled lava was then brought to a halt. The port of Haimaey was therefore saved.

In 1973, with pipes and unceasing labor the lava flows that were advancing toward the port of Heimaey in Iceland were cooled with seawater. For once, technology got the better of a volcano.

Volcanoes of the World and Elsewhere

> *The Roman poet Lucretius believed that Etna was hollow. Inside, he said, blows a hot, violent wind, which from time to time ejects stone and smoke. For the Sicilians who lived with it, Etna was quite simply the gateway to hell. For the Greeks, the volcano sheltered the forges of the god Hephaestus (he was Vulcan to the Romans, which is the origin of the word* **volcano.***)*

Centuries later, in 1716, the Frenchman Benoist de Maillet tried a first scientific explanation by assuming that the fire that came out of the mouth of volcanoes was caused by the combustion of animal fats concentrated in certain areas of the crust. In 1780, the Scotsman James Hutton came near the truth by supposing the existence of a fluid mass in the interior of the earth and compared volcanoes to safety valves that allowed the release of the excess molten materials.

The real explanation is simpler: coming from the upper mantle (at 100 to 300

kilometers (65 to 190 miles) depth), molten rocks under pressure (*magma*) try to push their way to the surface, attracted by weaker pressure. Fissures are then created in the hard rock of the crust at points of weakness. At 4 to 5 kilometers (2.5 to 3 miles) reservoirs are created, called "magmatic chambers," from which the magma continues its upward migration toward the surface. An eruption takes place when it reaches this point, leading to the formation of a volcano, as was the case of Paricutin in Mexico in 1943. If a volcanic cone already exists, only the "reawakening" of the volcano occurs. It may happen that the vent has been so clogged since the preceding eruption that an extraordinary amount of

Magma erupting from the terrestrial crust in the southern part of Lake Turkana in Kenya formed Nabocyaton, some tens of thousands of years ago.

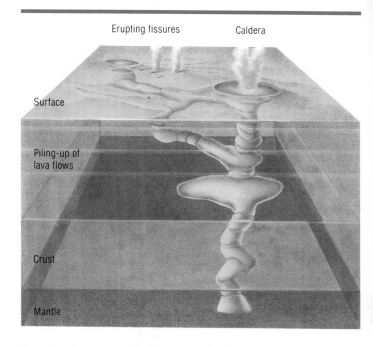

Erupting fissures

Caldera

Surface

Piling-up of lava flows

Crust

Mantle

The volcanic system of the Hawaiian islands: cross section of its internal structure.

energy accumulated there, which in the end blows off the peak of the volcano. This is what happened to Krakatoa, for instance, in 1883, and to Mount Saint Helens more recently, in 1980.

When the magmatic chamber, which is, as it were, the reservoir of the volcano, has emptied, the volcano subsides and becomes dormant. Molten material from the mantle then feeds the reservoir again, which, once it is filled, can cause a new eruption. This process sometimes takes several centuries. These successive fillings of the reservoir explain the intermittent activity of volcanoes. It can also happen that the magmatic chamber is no longer being fed. Then we have a really extinct volcano.

At the bottom of the Gulf of Tadjoura (Djibouti territory), a ridge rises from the ocean: here Africa and Asia separate.

Volcanic rocks

Basalt *is the most widespread of volcanic rocks, making up 90% of them. The lava that forms these rocks comes from a magmatic reservoir situated at a few kilometers' depth beneath the volcano — 3 kilometers (2 miles) for Stromboli, 5 kilometers (3 miles) for Vesuvius, and 20 kilometers (12 miles) for Etna. It is stored there for years, centuries, and sometimes even thousands of years. This rock contains iron, aluminum, calcium, magnesium, and particularly silica. If the proportion of silica is less than 50%, the lava is dense and black. Above 65% it is a ground mass with crystals and is pink. Between the two, it is gray and called andesite. Obsidian, which is black, is sometimes called volcanic glass. Its fragments are sharp. The Incas, for instance, used it to make cutting tools.*
Pumice stone *is the "froth" of lava. It is a whitish rock with numerous cavities caused by the presence of gas bubbles that escaped as it solidified. This is the reason for its low density. Countless pumice stones float in the Mediterranean, all around the Lipari*

The Ring of Fire

Let us look at a map of the distribution of volcanoes. It is very quickly apparent that most volcanoes are located around the Pacific Ocean, forming what is called the "ring of fire." This is because volcanoes are formed just above the site where one lithospheric plate sinks under another, as is the case with the Pacific plate. This plate is in fact growing in surface area because of the creation of a new ocean floor, along its ridge. The plate therefore attempts to sink under the Americas on one side and under Asia and Oceania on the other. This is

Head sculpted in basalt by the Olmecs (Mexico).

islands that shelter Stromboli. We should also mention rhyolite, an extremely hard rock, used mainly in Europe for ballast on railroad tracks.

why volcanoes are so numerous in Indonesia, Japan, Alaska, the Rocky Mountains, Central America, and the Andes. As the plate is consumed in the hot asthenosphere, the least dense part of the molten material rises and spreads at the surface. Such volcanoes form island arcs as in Japan, Indonesia and the West Indies. Volcanoes also occur all along ridges where, as previously mentioned, fresh material rising from the mantle spreads slowly at the surface on either side of a kind of lip. As nearly all the ridges are immersed in the oceans, these are submarine volcanoes: 10,000 can be counted in the Pacific Ocean alone, reaching more than 1000 meters (3000 feet) high; about 100 of them are active! They produce 15 cubic kilometers of new material a year. The water does not extinguish them, as might be thought, because there is no fire properly speaking, but rather extrusion of molten rocks, which cool. The big difference from volcanoes on continents is that the strong pressure of the water (several hundred times more than atmospheric pressure) prevents them from exploding.

Some submarine volcanoes, however, do become high enough to reach the surface. Then a column of water vapor spurts from the ocean (as did Surtsey, in Iceland, in 1963) and a new island appears. The archipelago of the Azores, for instance, or the island of Saint Helena where Napoleon I was exiled, are submarine volcanoes that have risen to the surface.

Between Plates

The lastly category includes volcanoes with no relation to the displacement of continental plates or the formation of ocean ridges. In fact, these volcanoes are located in the very middle of one of the seven large plates of the terrestrial crust and because of this are called "intraplate volcanoes." They are produced by columns of magma that have risen just enough to break through the terrestrial crust, in the same way that a bubble breaks on the surface of a pond.

If the plate is a continent, then you get volcanic systems like the Hoggar in the Sahara or the Massif Central in France. If the plate is an ocean (as is the Pacific, which is the only submerged plate), a highly imposing volcanic complex, like Hawaii, results.

In the case of Africa, a continent that has hardly moved in 30 million years, successive volcanoes are superposed since the hot spot is fixed. The Pacific plate, on the contrary, does move, and the hot spot generates a string of volcanoes that become dormant as it moves on. In any case, the American geologist James Dana noticed, as early as 1838, that the age of the

The circle is the main geometric form of volcanic peaks, *because ejected materials arrange themselves fairly uniformly around their source. This is a volcano in Kenya.*

Hawaiian volcanoes increases from the southeast to the northwest, along the axis of the chain, starting with the presently active volcanoes.

By means mainly of infrared detectors of space satellites, a total of 122 hot spots have been inventoried on the earth's surface, 69 of them continental and 53 submarine. Africa, by itself, possesses almost two-thirds of these continental hot spots. It must be said that this kind of volcanism is minor—less than 5% of the total number of volcanoes. In addition, very few of these volcanoes are active; only about ten of the hot spots have shown any degree of activity over the past 10 million years.

The geysers of Yellowstone

A geyser is a kind of subterranean kettle created by the infiltration of rainwater through a natural reservoir heated by a buried volcano. The area of Yellowstone in Wyoming represents indeed a subterranean volcanic zone. A reservoir of magma, located at a depth of 6 kilometers (4 miles), heats everything above it. Certain pockets of subterranean water are thus turned into steam. This steam forces its way to the surface and suddenly gushes out, at the same time becoming liquid again because of the lower pressure. At Yellowstone there are some 200 geysers. The highest, "Steamboat," is some 120 meters (360 feet) high, and the most regular is "Old Faithful," which gushes to a height of 60 meters (180 feet) for 3 or 4 minutes every hour. Geysers exist elsewhere, notably in Iceland and New Zealand. There are 400 in the world; half of them are at Yellowstone. The most powerful at one time was Waimangu, in New Zealand, which was active from 1900 to 1904: it sent 800 tons of water 450 meters (1400 feet) high every 30 hours, accompanied by an enormous din.

This schematic representation of some of the geysers of Yellowstone Park in the United States shows that they are truly underground kettles. Heated by a deep pocket of volcanic magma, infiltrated waters (arrows pointing down) rise toward the surface where they form huge jets of steam.

Porous rock

Heated rock

Magma

The Volcanic Kitchen

The lava that erupts from volcanoes varies in chemical composition, depending on which of the three above-mentioned categories they belong to. It is as if a cook were varying the proportions of the ingredients for a dish. The proportion of silica in the magma is critical, because the degree of viscosity of the lava, which itself regulates the type of eruption, depends on it. When lava contains more than 70% silica, it is viscous; with less than 50%, it is fluid.

Volcanologists distinguish four great types of eruption:

Hawaiian when the lava is fluid and spreads in broad flows, often through large fissures

Strombolian when equally broad flows are accompanied by explosions

Hawaiian-type eruption. *Fluid lava spreads as broad flows. The Hawaiian archipelago, the type model, is the largest volcanic complex on earth.*

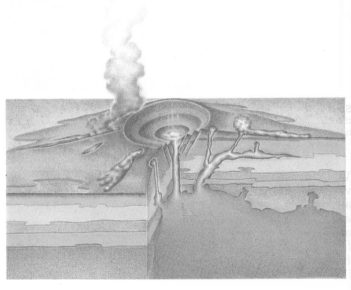

Strombolian-type eruption. *Type model: Stromboli, in the Lipari islands in the north of Sicily. Lava flows are broad and ejections are of an explosive nature.*

Vulcanian when the lava is viscous and hardly flows at all but violent ejections of ash and blocks spread above the volcano in the form of a mushroom cloud *Pelean* if the exit of the vent is blocked by plugs: under pressure from the gases, the plug rises and builds a dome that thickens at the top; pyroclastic flows (*nuées ardentes*) then escape through lateral fissures, burying broad surfaces under incandescent

A Vulcanian-type eruption. *Type model: Vulcano in the north of Sicily. There is little or no flow, but notice ejected blocks falling symmetrically from a mushroom cloud.*

materials. This type of volcano is very dangerous.

To be inclusive we must also mention collapsed volcanoes, formed by the subsidence of the summit after the magma reservoir has been partially or com-pletely emptied. The volcano then becomes a *caldera* (a Portuguese word meaning cauldron). This cauldron may attain gigan-tic dimensions—20 kilome-ters (12 miles) in Aso, the widest of the volcanoes active today. Even larger dimensions have been measured for extinct volcanoes, now worn down by erosion—100 kilometers (62 miles), a record, for the caldera of Toba on the island of Samosir near Sumatra. It must have erupted in a gigantic explosion about 75,000 years ago. Then there's Garita in the United States, Kari Kari in Bolivia, and Cerro Galon in Argentina.

Every volcanic crater of more than 1500 meters (4500 feet) in diameter is called a caldera. The caldera of the Piton de la Fournaise, on Réunion, is not circular. It measures 11 by 6 kilometers (7 by 4 miles). By comparison, the

Pelean-type eruption. *Type model: Montagne Pelée in Martinique. The very viscous lava causes plugs to form that increase pressure in the vent. The latter then explodes violently, generating pyroclastic flows (nuées ardentes).*

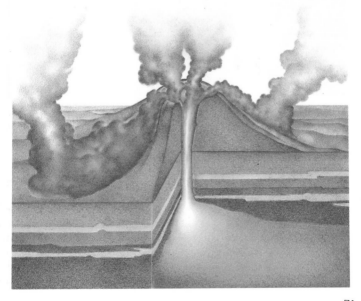

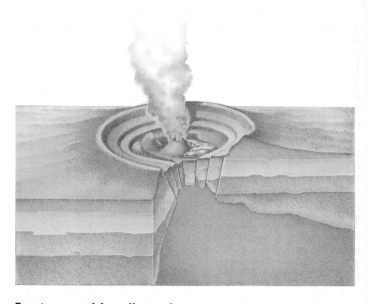

Eruption caused by collapse. *A succession of concentric calderas are formed, often with a spewing of ash and gas.*

mouth of Vesuvius is only 600 meters (1800 feet) in diameter.

Volcanoes by the Thousands

It is very difficult to account for all the volcanoes on earth. For one thing, a great number of them are under the sea, and the cartography of the ocean floors is not as easily achieved as that of the continents. Then again, no one is quite certain whether certain volcanoes are extinct or merely dormant. Roughly speaking, volcanologists estimate that there are 40,000 volcanoes on earth, three quarters of them under the oceans! Of the 10,000 continental volcanoes, 550 are active today and two of three belong to the Pacific ring of fire. A volcano is considered active if it has erupted at least once in historical times.

At any moment there are, somewhere on the surface of the earth, at least ten active volcanoes, spewing out lava and ash. As for eruptions, at least 20 can be counted each year. In all, 6000 eruptions have been observed over history.

The largest volcanic complex existing on the surface of our planet is that of Hawaii, which has a really fantastic volume; 50,000 cubic kilometers of lava. The diameter of the whole complex reaches 250 kilometers at the sea floor and 100 kilometers at the surface. Mauna Loa, the highest volcano of this chain, measured from the floor of the Pacific, is more even than Everest, the highest terrestrial peak. The highest continental volcano is Kilimanjaro, an intraplate volcano formed by a hot spot in Kenya. This volcano, with a volume ten times smaller than the Hawaiian complex but ten times greater than Etna, is at the moment dormant. Some volcanoes of the Andean cordillera, such as the dormant Nevado Ojos del Salado or the active Llullaillaco in Chile, are higher than Kilimanjaro, but since they are supported by a mountain range their real height is much less.

Volcanoes Beyond the Earth

The earth is not the only body of the solar system to have volcanoes.

Volcanoes were first discovered on the surface of the planet Mars in photographs from space probes. The largest, Nix Olympica, has dimensions that are considerable for a small planet like Mars. Probably this monster was able to increase in size above a hot spot comparable to those discovered on earth because the Martian crust does not move. At any rate, Nix Olympica, which has probably been extinct for a million years, is part of a complex containing other smaller volcanoes, also extinct. There are also strong indications that active volcanoes exist on the surface of Venus, especially in the mountainous region called "Beta Regio." Unfortunately, the thick mass of clouds that covers this planet prevents their direct observation.

Finally, to everyone's sur-

The fascinating work of volcanologists

A certain number of researchers remain permanently on the slopes of the earth's volcanoes, both to study them and to try to forecast their next awakening, while they are still dormant. Catastrophes must be avoided. For this purpose a large number of scientific instruments are deployed around the most dangerous volcanoes. These instruments register the slightest tremors and the least release of gases: seismographs for earthquakes caused by magma rising in the vent and tiltmeters and laser telemeters to measure (to the exact millimeter) the swelling of slopes under the thrust of the magma. The first volcano to be thus equipped was Kilauea, in the Hawaiian islands. Since then volcanological observatories have multiplied; there are now fifteen of them around the world, two important ones on the slopes of Etna and on the Piton de la Fournaise on Réunion. The measurements and observations that they collect help in the understanding of volcanic phenomena as well as in forecasting the renewal of eruptions.

This volcanologist *is collecting a molten basalt sample from the flow for chemical analysis.*

prise, active volcanoes have appeared on pictures taken by probes that flew over Io, one of the four main satellites of Jupiter. The largest, Ra Patera, has flows 200 kilometers (125 miles) long and a caldera 50 kilometers (30 miles) in diameter. Eight active volcanoes have been photographed on this satellite, which is hardly bigger than our moon, but it has in all more than 200 volcanoes.

And so we see that volcanoes are obviously not a rarity in the solar system, and that the study of the volcanoes of outer space will open a new chapter in volcanology.

This lava flow *is not on the earth but on Io, one of Jupiter's satellites. Ra Patera is one of the eight active volcanoes photographed on this little satellite.*

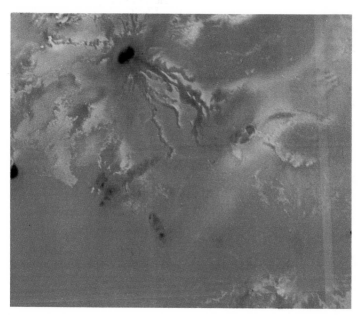

Index

Volcanoes and Earthquakes

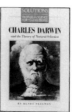